MW00760170

BOUND FOR GLORY
Five Patriotic Quilts

Nancy J. Martin

Martingale®
& COMPANY

Bound for Glory:
Five Patriotic Quilts
© 2007 by Nancy J. Martin

That Patchwork Place® is an imprint of
Martingale & Company®.

Martingale & Company
20205 144th Ave. NE
Woodinville, WA 98072-8478
www.martingale-pub.com

No part of this product may be reproduced
in any form, unless otherwise stated, in which
case reproduction is limited to the use of the
purchaser. The written instructions, photographs,
designs, projects, and patterns are intended for
the personal, noncommercial use of the retail
purchaser and are under federal copyright laws;
they are not to be reproduced by any electronic,
mechanical, or other means, including informa-
tional storage or retrieval systems, for commercial
use. Permission is granted to photocopy patterns
for the personal use of the retail purchaser.
Attention teachers: Martingale & Company
encourages you to use this book for teaching,
subject to the restrictions stated above.

    The information in this book is presented in
good faith, but no warranty is given nor results
guaranteed. Since Martingale & Company has no
control over choice of materials or procedures,
the company assumes no responsibility for the
use of this information.

Printed in China
12 11 10 09 08 07   8 7 6 5 4 3 2 1

Library of Congress Cataloging-in-Publication Data
Library of Congress Control Number: 2006035749

ISBN: 978-1-56477-737-9

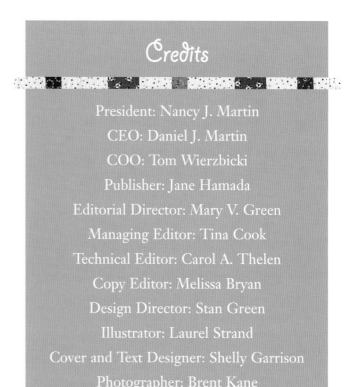

Credits

President: Nancy J. Martin

CEO: Daniel J. Martin

COO: Tom Wierzbicki

Publisher: Jane Hamada

Editorial Director: Mary V. Green

Managing Editor: Tina Cook

Technical Editor: Carol A. Thelen

Copy Editor: Melissa Bryan

Design Director: Stan Green

Illustrator: Laurel Strand

Cover and Text Designer: Shelly Garrison

Photographer: Brent Kane

Mission Statement

Dedicated to providing quality products
and service to inspire creativity.

Contents

Introduction 4

Quiltmaking Techniques 5

Projects
Paper Pinwheels 8

Carrie Nation 11

Sergeant's Chevron 14

Union 18

Liberty Star 22

Introduction

What's not to like about a red-white-and-blue quilt? One of the owners of the Heirloom Quilts shop in Poulsbo, Washington, made that comment as I purchased patriotic prints one day, and I realized how true her words are—everyone enjoys a quilt of red, white, and blue.

Although this book includes quilts done in bright shades of red, white, and blue, I also explored muted variations of these colors. The choice is yours! There's a great availability of patriotic prints right now, but then they've always been a popular fabric option in quilt shops. So, if the particular prints that I used in *Bound for Glory* are no longer available, don't worry—there will be new selections to take their places.

The projects in this book fill a variety of needs. I refer to the first three as "double-time" quilts, because each is easy to make in a day or weekend. If adding to your holiday decor is a goal, consider hanging a *Bound for Glory* quilt on Presidents' Day, Memorial Day, Flag Day, Independence Day, or Veterans Day.

If you're interested in showing appreciation for a member of the armed services, there are several "Soldier Quilt" groups that distribute quilts. Any of the *Bound for Glory* quilts would be ideal for one of these organizations. Two are listed below.

Quilts of Valor Foundation
www.qovf.org
(509) 346-9332

Soldiers' Angels
www.soldiersangels.org
(615) 676-0239

I've written many quilting books that contain complete, start-to-finish quiltmaking instructions. You probably have some of these types of books to use for reference. Here, I'll just review the special techniques I've used to make the projects in this book.

Basic Bias-Square Technique

Many traditional quilt patterns contain squares made from two contrasting half-square triangles. The short sides of the triangles are on the straight grain of fabric while the long sides are on the bias. These are called bias squares. Using a bias-strip-piecing method, you can easily sew and cut large amounts of bias squares. This technique is especially useful for small bias squares, where pressing after stitching usually distorts the shape (and sometimes burns fingers).

Note: All directions in this book give the cut size for bias squares; the finished size after stitching will be ½" smaller.

1. To make just a few bias squares, start with two small squares of fabric. The directions in this book call for a pair of 8" x 8" squares. Layer with right sides together and cut in half diagonally.

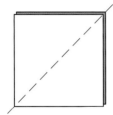

2. Cut into strips, measuring from the previous cut.

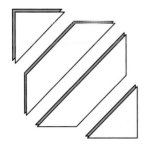

3. Stitch the strips together using ¼"-wide seam allowances. Be sure to align the strips so that the lower edge and one adjacent edge form straight lines. Always press the seams toward the darker fabric.

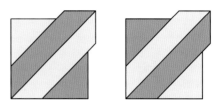

4. Starting at the lower-left corner, align the 45° mark of a square ruler such as a Bias Square® on the seam line. Each bias square will require two cuts. The first cut is along one side and the top edge. It removes the bias square from the rest of the fabric and is made slightly larger than the correct size, as shown in the following illustrations.

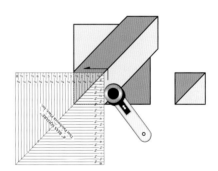

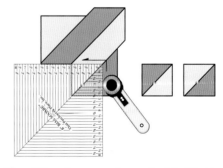

Align 45° mark on seam line and cut first 2 sides.

5. The second cut is made along the remaining two sides. It aligns the diagonal and trims the bias square to the correct size. To make the cut, turn the segment and place the ruler on the opposite two sides, aligning the required measurements on both sides of the cutting guide and the 45° mark on the seam. Cut the remaining two sides of the bias squares.

Turn cut segments and cut opposite 2 sides.

Borders with Butted Corners

The easiest border to add is one with butted corners. You will save fabric if you stitch the border to the longest sides first, and then stitch the border to the remaining two sides.

1. Measure the length of the quilt through the center. Cut two border strips to this measurement.

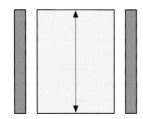

Measure center of quilt, top to bottom.

If you cut borders on the crosswise grain, you may need to piece strips together before adding them to the quilt. The seam will be less noticeable and stronger if it is pieced on an angle. You may need additional fabric to do so.

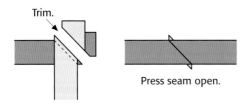

Trim.

Press seam open.

2. Mark the centers of the border strips and the quilt top. Pin the borders to the sides of the quilt, matching centers and ends and easing or slightly stretching the quilt to fit the border strip as necessary.

3. Sew the side borders in place and press the seams toward the borders.

4. Measure the center width of the quilt, including the side borders, to determine the length of the top and bottom borders. Cut two border strips to this measurement, piecing strips as necessary. Mark, pin, sew in place, and press the top and bottom border strips in the same way you attached the side borders.

Borders with Mitered Corners

Mitered borders have a diagonal seam where the borders meet in the corners. If your quilt has multiple borders, sew together all the border strips for the sides, top, and bottom, and treat each resulting unit as a single border.

1. Mark the center of each quilt edge and each border strip.

2. Measure the length and width of the quilt top through the center.

3. Place a pin at each end of the side borders to mark the length of the quilt top. Repeat with the top and bottom borders to mark the width.

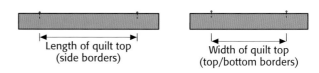

Length of quilt top
(side borders)

Width of quilt top
(top/bottom borders)

4. Pin the side borders to the quilt top, matching the centers. Line up the pins at either end of the border strips with the quilt edges. Stitch, beginning and ending the stitching ¼" from the raw edges of the quilt top. Repeat with the remaining borders.

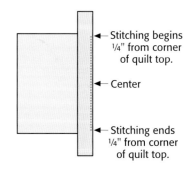

Stitching begins ¼" from corner of quilt top.

Center

Stitching ends ¼" from corner of quilt top.

5. Lay the first corner to be mitered on the ironing board. Fold under one border at a 45° angle to the other. Press and pin.

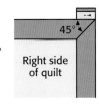

6. Fold the quilt with right sides together, lining up the edges of the border. If necessary, use a ruler and pencil to draw a line on the crease to make the line more visible. Stitch on the pressed crease, sewing from the corner to the outside edges.

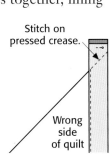

7. Trim the excess from the borders, leaving a ¼"-wide seam allowance. Press the seam open. Repeat with the remaining corners.

Bias Binding

A double-layer bias binding rolls over the edges of a quilt nicely, and the two layers of fabric resist wear. If you use 2¼"-wide strips, the finished width of this binding will be ⅜".

Double-layer French binding

After quilting, trim excess batting and backing even with the edge of the quilt top. A rotary cutter and long ruler will ensure accurate straight edges. If the basting is no longer in place, baste all three layers together at the outer edges.

1. Cut 2¼"-wide bias strips; each project specifies the total length of strips needed.

2. Stitch the bias strips together, offsetting them as shown. Press the seams open.

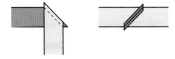

3. Fold the strip in half lengthwise, wrong sides together, and press.

4. Unfold the binding at one end and turn under ¼" at a 45° angle as shown.

5. Beginning on a side of the quilt, stitch the binding to the quilt, using a ¼"-wide seam allowance. Start stitching 1" to 2" from the beginning of the binding. Stop stitching ¼" from the corner and backstitch.

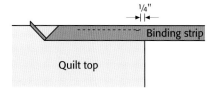

6. Turn the quilt to prepare for sewing along the next edge. Fold the binding away from the quilt as shown, and then fold again to align the binding with the edge of the quilt to create an angled pleat at the corner.

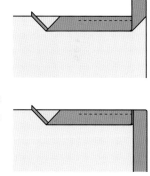

7. Stitch from the fold of the binding along the edge of the quilt top, stopping ¼" from the corner as you did for the first corner; backstitch. Repeat the stitching and mitering process on the remaining edges and corners of the quilt.

8. When you reach the beginning of the binding, cut the end 1" longer than needed and tuck the end inside the beginning. Stitch the rest of the binding.

9. Turn the binding to the back, over the raw edges of the quilt. Blindstitch in place, covering the machine stitching. At each corner, fold the binding as shown to form a miter before stitching it to the quilt back.

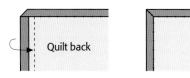

Paper Pinwheels

Two types of pinwheels can be seen in this bright red-white-and-blue quilt: the large red pinwheel in the center of each block and the navy pinwheel that is formed when the blocks are sewn together. Hang this happy quilt on Independence Day.

20 blocks, set 4 across and 5 down

Materials and Cutting

Yardage is based on 42"-wide fabric. All measurements include ¼"-wide seam allowances.

10 fat eighths of assorted red fabrics. From *each*, cut:
1 square, 8" x 8", for bias squares (10 total)
2 squares, 4½" x 4½", for blocks (20 total)

5 fat eighths of white background fabrics. From *each*, cut:
16 squares, 2½" x 2½", for blocks (80 total)

1¾ yards of navy print. Cut:
10 squares, 8" x 8", for bias squares
110 squares, 2½" x 2½", for blocks and sashing
6 strips, 2¾" x 42", for outer border

1 yard of striped fabric. Cut:
49 pieces, 2½" x 8½", for sashing

3 yards of fabric for backing

½ yard of striped fabric for bias binding

Batting, 50" x 60"

Selecting Fabric

I enjoy using a variety of fabrics in my quilts to create a more interesting look. My motto has always been, "Why use 2 fabrics, when you can use 20?" If you work with scraps or fat quarters, you can use a number of different fabrics to represent a single value.

Sort your fabrics or scraps into color families of red, white, and blue. Select a whole range of fabrics; begin with dark navy blues, adding royal blues and medium blues. Make sure that the red fabrics also span a wide range of colors from bright red to reddish orange. The white color family can contain bright whites, cream, ivory, and beige prints.

Directions

1. Pair the red 8" and navy 8" squares, referring to the directions for bias squares on page 5. Cut each square into 2½"-wide strips, and then stitch and cut 80 bias squares, 2½" x 2½".

By Nancy J. Martin, Kingston, Washington, 2005.
Quilted by Jacque Noard, Kingston, Washington.

Finished Size: 47" x 57" • Block Size: 8" x 8"

2. Arrange the bias squares, white squares, navy squares, and a red square into rows, and then stitch the rows together to make a block. Make 20.

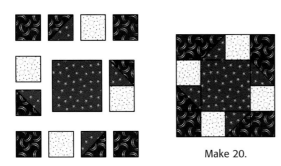

Make 20.

3. Join four blocks and five striped sashing strips to make a row. Make five rows of blocks.

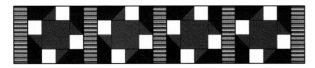

Make 5.

4. Join four sashing strips and five navy squares to make a row. Make six rows of sashing.

Make 6.

5. Stitch the rows of blocks and sashing together to form the quilt top.

6. Add the navy 2¾"-wide border strips, referring to the directions on page 6 for "Borders with Butted Corners."

7. Mark the quilt top with the design of your choice. The quilt pictured here was quilted in the ditch of each seam. Layer with batting and backing. Baste. Hand or machine quilt as desired.

8. Referring to "Bias Binding" on page 7, cut 2¼"-wide bias strips from the striped binding fabric. Make a total of 218" of bias binding and sew it to the quilt.

Carrie Nation

Carrie Nation was a crusader for the Woman's Christian Temperance Union during the early 1900s. She terrorized bars and saloons with a hatchet, fighting for prohibition of alcohol. The block that carries her name is easy to stitch, and devoid of the terror Carrie Nation created.

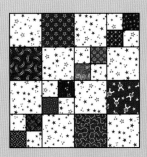

24 blocks, set 4 across and 6 down

Materials and Cutting

Yardage is based on 42"-wide fabric. All measurements include ¼"-wide seam allowances.

6 fat quarters of assorted red fabrics. From *each*, cut:

16 squares, 3½" x 3½", for blocks (96 total)

6 fat quarters of assorted blue fabrics. From *each*, cut:

3 strips, 2" x 22", for blocks; cut an extra strip from *2* of the blue fabrics (20 total)

2½ yards of white background fabric. Cut:

192 squares, 3½" x 3½", for blocks

20 strips, 2" x 22"

3 yards of fabric for backing

½ yard of red fabric for bias binding

Batting, 52" x 76"

Selecting Background Fabrics

First look to see if your quilt pattern has a "background" on which a design will appear. Most quilts do. If so, select your background fabric first. Don't limit your choices to solid colors. Remember, solid-colored fabrics tend to emphasize mismatched seams and irregular quilting stitches. If you are a beginner and are still perfecting your piecing and quilting skills, select a print that is more likely to hide minor imperfections.

Prints with a white background have a clean, formal look; those with a beige or tan background resemble antique quilts and have a more informal look. Once you have chosen the background fabric, select the remaining fabrics to enhance the background fabric.

Directions

1. Stitch each blue strip to a white strip along the long edges. Make 20 strip sets. Cut each set into 2"-wide segments for a total of 192 segments.

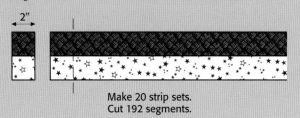

Make 20 strip sets.
Cut 192 segments.

11

By Nancy J. Martin and Cleo Nollette, Kingston, Washington, 2005.
Quilted by Jacque Noard, Kingston, Washington.

Finished Size: 48" x 72" • Block Size: 12" x 12"

2. Stitch segments together in pairs to make 96 four-patch units.

Make 96.

3. Arrange the four-patch units, red squares, and white squares into rows, and then stitch the rows together to make a block. Make 24.

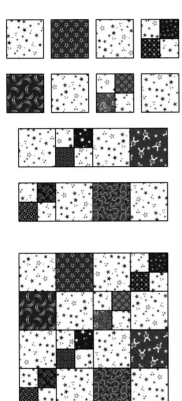

Make 24.

4. Join four blocks to make a row. Make six rows, arranging the blocks as shown.

Make 6.

5. Stitch the rows of blocks together to form the quilt top.

6. Mark the quilt top with the design of your choice. The quilt shown is quilted using continuous curves alongside each seam line. Layer with batting and backing. Baste. Hand or machine quilt as desired.

7. Referring to "Bias Binding" on page 7, cut 2¼"-wide bias strips from the red binding fabric. Make a total of 250" of bias binding and sew it to the quilt.

Sergeant's Chevron

Sergeant's Chevron mimics the stripes on a sergeant's uniform and on the Boy Scout uniform. The finished quilt can be used to display military patches and awards or scout badges. Colorful pinwheels add an energizing border.

6 blocks, set diagonally 2 across and 3 down

Materials and Cutting

Yardage is based on 42"-wide fabric. All measurements include ¼"-wide seam allowances.

1 yard of red fabric. Cut:

6 strips, 1½" x 42", for chevrons

12 squares, 8" x 8", for bias squares

1 yard of white background fabric. Cut:

3 squares, 5⅞" x 5⅞"; cut once diagonally to make 6 triangles for blocks

4 strips, 1½" x 42", for chevrons

12 squares, 8" x 8", for bias squares

2¼ yards of navy fabric. Cut:

9 squares, 5⅞" x 5⅞"; cut once diagonally to make 18 triangles for blocks

2 squares, 15½" x 15½"; cut twice diagonally to make 8 setting triangles. (You will have 2 extra.)

2 squares, 8" x 8"; cut once diagonally to make 4 corner setting triangles

2 squares, 10½" x 10½", for setting squares

11 squares, 8⅜" x 8⅜"; cut twice diagonally to make 44 large triangles for border

4 squares, 4½" x 4½"; cut once diagonally to make 8 small triangles for top and bottom borders

6 strips, 2½" x 42", for outer border

1 fat quarter of yellow fabric. Cut:

6 appliqué stars using the pattern on page 17

3 yards of fabric for backing

½ yard of striped fabric for bias binding

Batting, 52" x 64"

Directions

1. Stitch a white triangle to a navy triangle of the same size. Then, beginning with a red strip, stitch strips Log Cabin–style to the two unsewn sides of the white triangle and trim strips as shown. Continue sewing strips, alternating the red and white strips and ending with a red strip.

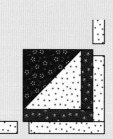

By Nancy J. Martin, Kingston, Washington, 2005.
Quilted by Jacque Noard, Kingston, Washington.

Finished Size: 47¾" x 60¾" • Block Size: 10" x 10"

2. Align the 45° angle of a square ruler such as a Bias Square along the seam line between the white triangle and the first red strip, and align the ¼" line along the seam between the navy and white triangles as shown. Trim the side of the block to square it up. Repeat for the other side.

 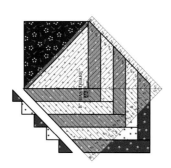

3. Stitch a navy 5⅞" triangle to the two long sides of each chevron design to complete the block. Make six.

4. Appliqué a yellow star to each block using your favorite method. Refer to the tip box "Appliqué" on page 17 for more detailed appliqué information.

5. Arrange the blocks, setting squares, setting triangles, and corner setting triangles into diagonal rows. Sew the rows together.

6. Pair the red 8" and white 8" squares, referring to the directions for bias squares on page 5. Cut each square into 2¾"-wide strips, and then stitch and cut 96 bias squares, 3" x 3".

7. Join four bias squares to make a Pinwheel block. Make 24.

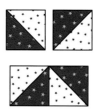

Make 24.

8. Join four Pinwheel blocks, two small navy triangles, and six large navy triangles to make the top border. Repeat to make the bottom border. Stitch the borders to the quilt.

Make 2.

9. Join six Pinwheel blocks and 12 large navy triangles to make a side border. Make two. Stitch the side borders to the quilt.

10. Join a Pinwheel block, two large navy triangles, and one small navy triangle to make a corner block. Make four.

Make 4.

11. Stitch the corner blocks to the quilt top.

12. Add the 2½"-wide navy border strips, referring to the directions on page 6 for "Borders with Butted Corners."

13. Mark the quilt top with the design of your choice. The quilt shown is quilted in the ditch for the patchwork, and the background is quilted with stipple meandering. Layer with batting and backing. Hand or machine quilt as desired.

14. Referring to "Bias Binding" on page 7, cut 2¼"-wide bias strips from the striped binding fabric. Make a total of 228" of bias binding and sew it to the quilt.

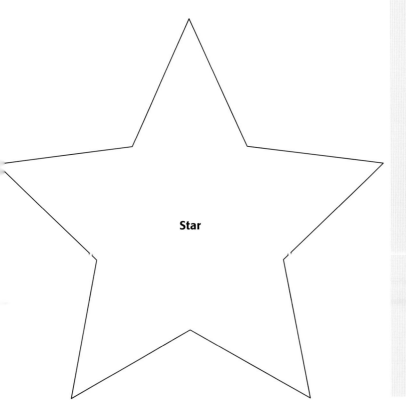

Star

Appliqué

1. Make a stiffened template of each shape in the appliqué design on bond-weight paper. Do not add seam allowances to the templates.

2. Pin the paper to the wrong side of the fabric.

3. Cut out the fabric shapes, adding ⅛"-wide seam allowances around each paper shape.

Wrong side of fabric

4. With your fingers, turn the seam allowances over the edge of the paper and baste the fabric to the paper. Clip the corners, doing inside curves first. (A little clipping may be necessary to help the fabric stretch.) On outside curves, take small running stitches through the fabric only, to ease in fullness.

5. For sharply pointed corners, such as the tips of the stars, first fold the corner to the inside, and then fold the remaining seam allowances over the paper.

Fold corners to inside.

Fold over remaining seam allowances.

6. Take an occasional stitch through the paper to hold the fabric in place. When all the seam allowances are turned and basted, press the appliqué pieces. Position and pin the pieces in place on the background fabric.

7. Use a small blind hem stitch and a single strand of matching thread to appliqué the shapes to the background fabric. Remove the basting stitches, cut a small slit on the back of the background fabric, and remove the paper.

Union

A delightful novelty print, depicting children marching with drums and flags, fills the center of each Union block in this quilt. The blocks are made in two different color schemes alternated between perky plaid sashing. Display this patriotic quilt on Flag Day.

9 blocks, set 3 across and 3 down

Materials and Cutting

Yardage is based on 42"-wide fabric. All measurements include ¼"-wide seam allowances.

1 fat quarter of theme print. Cut*:

9 squares, 4½" x 4½", for blocks

1¼ yards of beige background fabric. Cut:

9 squares, 8" x 8", for bias squares

9 squares, 5¼" x 5¼", for flying geese

36 squares, 2½" x 2½", for red blocks and blue blocks

1 fat eighth of deep red fabric. Cut:

8 squares, 3¾" x 3¾"; cut once diagonally to make 16 triangles for red blocks

⅝ yard of red star print. Cut:

4 squares, 8" x 8", for bias squares

16 squares, 2⅞" x 2⅞", for flying geese

8 squares, 2½" x 2½", for sashing squares

1 fat quarter of checked fabric. Cut:

8 squares, 4⅞" x 4⅞"; cut once diagonally to make 16 triangles for red blocks

½ yard of blue fabric. Cut:

10 squares, 3¾" x 3¾"; cut once diagonally to make 20 triangles for blue blocks

6 strips, 1½" x 42", for inner border

1 fat quarter of red striped fabric. (See "Cutting Stripes" on page 20.) Cut:

10 squares, 4⅞" x 4⅞"; cut once diagonally to make 20 triangles for blue blocks

⅝ yard of blue star print. Cut:

5 squares, 8" x 8", for bias squares

20 squares, 2⅞" x 2⅞", for flying geese

8 squares, 2½" x 2½", for sashing

⅝ yard of plaid fabric. Cut:

24 pieces, 2½" x 12½", for sashing

1¾ yards of striped fabric. Cut:

4 strips, 6" x 63", for outer border

3½ yards of fabric for backing

½ yard of striped fabric for bias binding

Batting, 64" x 64"

*You may need to purchase additional fabric to fussy cut the center squares.

By Cleo Nollette, Seattle, Washington, 2005.
Quilted by Jacque Noard, Kingston, Washington.

Finished Size: 57½" x 57½" • Block Size: 12" x 12"

Cutting Stripes

Controlling the direction of striped fabric or directional prints requires careful cutting and placement. When cutting half-square triangles, cut half the triangles in one direction and the other half in the opposite direction.

When sewing these pieces to a square or diamond, stitch the triangles cut in one direction to opposite sides of the center square.

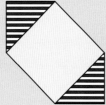

Next, sew the pieces cut in the opposite direction to the remaining sides of the center square.

Directions

1. Pair the beige and red star 8" squares, referring to the directions for bias squares on page 5. Cut each square into 2½"-wide strips, and then stitch and cut 32 bias squares, 2½" x 2½".

2. Stitch a deep red triangle to each side of a novelty-print square. Make four. Stitch four checked triangles to each unit.

3. Arrange two rows of two bias squares and one flying-geese unit each as shown and stitch to the top and bottom of each unit.

Flying-Geese Units

Using a large background square and four dark squares, you can make four flying-geese units at the same time. With right sides together, place two dark 2⅞" squares on one background 5¼" square as shown.

Using a ruler, draw a line diagonally from corner to corner. Stitch a scant ¼" on both sides of the drawn line. Cut apart on the drawn line.

Press the seam allowances toward the dark fabric. With right sides together, place a dark 2⅞" square on each unit and draw a diagonal line on the dark fabric as shown.

Stitch a scant ¼" on both sides of the drawn line. Cut apart on the drawn line and press the seam allowances toward the dark fabric.

4. Stitch the remaining bias squares and flying-geese along with the beige 2½" squares into two rows. Join to each side to complete the block. Make four blocks with this coloration.

Make 4.

5. To make five blue blocks, pair the remaining beige background squares with the blue star 8" squares and make 40 bias squares, 2½" x 2½", as in step 1. Stitch four blue triangles to each of the remaining novelty-print squares and then stitch four red striped triangles to each unit as in step 2. Complete the block as in steps 3 and 4, using the blue-and-beige bias squares, flying geese, and the remaining beige 2½" squares.

Make 5.

6. Lay out the red and blue blocks in three rows of three blocks each, alternating colors as shown. Position the plaid sashing strips between the blocks, and alternate the red star and blue star sashing squares, referring to the diagram. Sew the blocks and sashing pieces together into rows, and then sew the rows together.

7. Cut two of the blue 1½"-wide inner-border strips in half. Join a 1½"-wide half strip to a 1½"-wide whole strip. Repeat to make four border strips, approximately 63" long. Stitch each inner-border strip to a 6"-wide outer-border strip. Then follow the directions for "Borders with Mitered Corners" on page 6, treating each strip as a unit.

8. Mark the quilt top with the design of your choice. The quilt shown here was quilted with an allover design of loops, using thread that blended with the muted fabrics. Layer with batting and backing. Baste. Hand or machine quilt as desired.

9. Referring to "Bias Binding" on page 7, cut 2¼"-wide bias strips from the striped binding fabric. Make a total of 240" of binding and sew it to the quilt.

Liberty Star

The theme fabric for this muted patriotic quilt features old-fashioned urns draped in banners embellished with the words "Liberty," "Freedom," and "Peace." The quilt design appears when the quilt is set together in rows, rather than pieced from individual blocks.

Materials and Cutting

Yardage is based on 42"-wide fabric. All measurements include ¼"-wide seam allowances.

1 yard of theme print. Cut*:

3 squares, 10½" x 10½", for blocks

26 squares, 5½" x 5½", for blocks

1¼ yards of beige background fabric. Cut:

6 strips, 1½" x 42", for inner border

14 rectangles, 3" x 5½", for rows

4 squares, 3" x 3", for rows

36 squares, 3½" x 3½"; cut twice diagonally to make 144 large triangles for pieced border

4 squares, 2¼" x 2¼"; cut once diagonally to make 8 small triangles for pieced border

2 yards of blue print. Cut:

4 strips, 4¼" x 62", along the *lengthwise* grain, for outer border

68 squares, 3⅜" x 3⅜"; cut once diagonally to make 136 triangles for unit 2

I yard of muted red fabric. Cut:

25 squares, 4" x 4", for unit 1

66 squares, 2⅝" x 2⅝", for pieced border

3½ yards of fabric for backing

½ yard of blue fabric for bias binding

Batting, 62" x 71"

*You may need to purchase additional fabric to fussy cut the squares.

Using Theme Prints

Many theme or novelty prints require special cutting to show them to their best advantage. I take the time to fussy cut these fabrics for my quilts, knowing that the results are well worth the effort, even though the remaining fabric looks like a piece of Swiss cheese when I am finished.

To fussy cut a fabric, make an expandable window from two L-shaped pieces of cardboard. Place this window on the different design elements in the fabric, noting the size needed to accommodate each design. Look for a common size that will work for most of the designs; unfortunately, not all the motifs may be the same size. Once you determine a common size, add ¼"-wide seam allowances on all sides and cut the necessary pieces.

By Nancy J. Martin, Kingston, Washington, 2005.
Quilted by Frankie Schmitt, Kenmore, Washington.

Finished Size: 57½" x 66½"

Directions

1. Sew four blue triangles to a large muted red square to make unit 1. Make 25. Sew two blue triangles to a large beige triangle to make unit 2. Make 18.

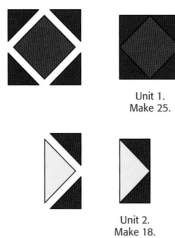

Unit 1.
Make 25.

Unit 2.
Make 18.

2. Arrange and sew units 1 and 2, big and small theme-print squares, and beige rectangles and squares together into rows as shown. Join the rows.

3. Cut two of the beige 1½"-wide inner-border strips in half. Join a 1½"-wide half strip to a 1½"-wide whole strip. Repeat to make four border strips, approximately 50" long. Add the inner borders, referring to the directions on page 6 for "Borders with Butted Corners."

4. Join 14 small muted red squares, 26 beige 3½" triangles, and 2 beige 2¼" triangles to make the top border. Repeat to make the bottom border. Join 17 small muted red squares and 33 beige 3½" triangles for each pieced side border. Sew the pieced top and bottom borders to the quilt top, and then add the pieced side borders.

Top/bottom border.
Make 2.

Side border.
Make 2.

5. Join two beige 3½" triangles and one beige 2¼" triangle to a small muted red square to make a corner triangle. Make four and stitch them to the corners of the quilt top.

Make 4.

6. Referring to "Borders with Butted Corners" on page 6, stitch the blue outer borders to the quilt top.

7. Mark the quilt top with the design of your choice. The quilt shown was quilted with continuous curves in the red squares and stipple meandering in the background. Layer with batting and backing. Baste. Hand or machine quilt as desired.

8. Referring to "Bias Binding" on page 7, cut 2¼"-wide strips from the blue fabric for binding. Make a total of 254" of binding and sew it to the quilt.